Instant Handlebars.js

Learn how to create and implement HTML templates into your projects using the Handlebars library

Gabriel Manricks

BIRMINGHAM - MUMBAI

Instant Handlebars.js

Copyright © 2013 Packt Publishing

All rights reserved. No part of this book may be reproduced, stored in a retrieval system, or transmitted in any form or by any means, without the prior written permission of the publisher, except in the case of brief quotations embedded in critical articles or reviews.

Every effort has been made in the preparation of this book to ensure the accuracy of the information presented. However, the information contained in this book is sold without warranty, either express or implied. Neither the author, nor Packt Publishing, and its dealers and distributors will be held liable for any damages caused or alleged to be caused directly or indirectly by this book.

Packt Publishing has endeavored to provide trademark information about all of the companies and products mentioned in this book by the appropriate use of capitals. However, Packt Publishing cannot guarantee the accuracy of this information.

First published: September 2013

Production Reference: 1240913

Published by Packt Publishing Ltd.
Livery Place
35 Livery Street
Birmingham B3 2PB, UK.

ISBN 978-1-78328-265-4

www.packtpub.com

Credits

Author
Gabriel Manricks

Reviewers
Jonathan Christopher
Nuno Oliveira

Acquisition Editor
Rubal Kaur

Commissioning Editor
Llewellyn Rozario

Technical Editor
Dipika Gaonkar

Project Coordinator
Sageer Parkar

Proofreader
Julie Blake

Production Coordinator
Aparna Bhagat

Cover Work
Aparna Bhagat

Cover Image
Sheetal Aute

About the Author

Gabriel Manricks is a full stack software & web developer focusing on PHP and both frontend and server-side JavaScript frameworks.

Gabriel works as a staff writer for NetTuts+, where he enjoys learning as well as teaching others, and he also freelances in web consulting, development, and writing.

About the Reviewers

Jonathan Christopher is a developer living in upstate New York with his wife Carrie and their son Micah. He focuses on both frontend and server-side development for his company Iron to Iron (http://irontoiron.com). He writes for *Monday By Noon* (http://mondaybynoon.com) and has also authored *Client Oriented WordPress Development* (https://clientwp.com).

Nuno Oliveira is a software engineer with over 10 years of professional experience. A windows developer for many years, he has an extensive background in the full life cycle of the software development process. He now concentrates on web development, working with ASP.net, PHP, HTML, CSS, and JavaScript. He currently lives in London, United Kingdom. You can always find him on twitter at @nm_oliveira.

www.PacktPub.com

Support files, e-Books, discount offers, and more

You might want to visit www.PacktPub.com for support files and downloads related to your book.

Did you know that Packt offers e-Book versions of every book published, with PDF and e-Pub files available? You can upgrade to the e-Book version at www.PacktPub.com and as a print book customer, you are entitled to a discount on the e-Book copy. Get in touch with us at service@packtpub.com for more details.

At www.PacktPub.com, you can also read a collection of free technical articles, sign up for a range of free newsletters, and receive exclusive discounts and offers on Packt books and e-Books.

packtlib.packtpub.com

Do you need instant solutions to your IT questions? PacktLib is Packt's online digital book library. Here, you can access, read, and search across Packt's entire library of books.

Why Subscribe?

- Fully searchable across every book published by Packt
- Copy and paste, print and bookmark content
- On demand and accessible via web browser

Free Access for Packt account holders

If you have an account with Packt at www.PacktPub.com, you can use this to access PacktLib today and view nine entirely free books. Simply use your login credentials for immediate access.

Table of Contents

Instant Handlebars.js — 1
So, what is Handlebars? — 3
The syntax — 3
Installation — 5
Downloading the Handlebars library — 5
Precompiling templates — 5
Quick start – creating your first template — 7
Preparing the project — 7
Block helpers — 8
Top 6 features you need to know about — 11
Expressions — 11
Helpers — 12
Partials — 29
Structuring a Handlebars app — 31
Precompilation — 38
Logging and comments — 45
People and places you should get to know — 47
Official sites — 47
Community — 47
Frameworks — 48
Twitter — 48
About Packt Publishing — 49
Writing for Packt — 49

Instant Handlebars.js

Welcome to the *Instant Handlebars.js*, in this book we will be taking a thorough look through this amazing templating library, as well as ways to manage your projects and optimize them for production.

This book contains the following sections:

So, what is Handlebars? here we will take a look at what a templating engine really is and more specifically why we are learning Handlebars.

Installation we will go through downloading the Handlebars library as-well as installing node.js and the handlebars CLI.

Quick start – creating your first template will get our feet wet, starting off by writing the minimum amount of code required to get a template onto the page, moving on to creating a simple helper.

Top 6 Features you need to know about will take a deep look at all the features Handlebars has to offer, as well as tips on organizing large projects and pre-compiling templates. Topics include:

- *Expressions*: These are the core of templates, and a good starting point to get comfortable with the library
- *Helpers*: These are where Handlebars gets its extendibility; we will look at all the different types of helpers and settings you have available
- *Partials*: These are the building blocks of the templating world, and they open the door for modular design
- *Structuring a Handlebars app*: In this section, we will take a look at a number of different ways to structure an app, pointing out the different pros and cons

- *Precompilation*: will continue to structure are projects, but with a focus on pre-compiling our resources for a more optimized and efficient site
- *Logging and comments*: The final section will be about writing clear and debug-able templates and helpers, so you can easily test and maintain them in the future.

People and places you should get to know will take a look at different people and places you should subscribe to, to stay up-to-date, and learn more.

So, what is Handlebars?

To answer this properly, we need to first understand what a templating engine is, or better, what it comes to accomplish. Any dynamic site (blog, store, and so on) has parts which remain static, and at least rules on how the dynamic data should be inserted. A templating engine can and should be thought of as a new language in its own right and has a specialized syntax made specifically for rendering views.

Before templating engines you would have some kind of code in your actual DOM pages, through which you would insert the dynamic pieces of data at specific points. This is not great code separation, and it's definitely not a very clean option. A templating engine is meant to augment this step with its specialized syntax made specifically for this purpose; if done right, you should end up with clean and reusable templates, and leave your app clear of any bodge code.

Mustache was a pretty popular templating library for years and has basically been ported to nearly every programming language available. The problem with Mustache is that it is fairly opinionated on how you should write your templates; it follows a strict "View-Controller" separation and is a purely logic-less engine made specifically for replacing expressions with pre-computed data. Handlebars is a superset of the Mustache library, that adds a lot of logic and extensibility, making it a more flexible solution, while still retaining full backward compatibility, so that any Mustache templates can work out of the box. Following are the features of Handlebars:

- It has a very simple and easy to write syntax
- It allows you to add some logic using helpers but still separates it from the actual template's code to keep them easy to manage
- It's very fast and allows you to pre-compile your templates in JavaScript

Because of this, Handlebars has become the premier choice when it comes to frontend templates and is currently being used in many of the popular frameworks such as Meteor and Ember.js.

Not to mention the fact that it was built by the legendary *Yehuda Katz*, who is a core member on projects such as, jQuery, Ruby on Rails, and the Ember.js framework.

The syntax

I have been speaking about Handlebars "specialized" syntax for a bit now, and about how it was made specifically for views. Basically, every command or option in Handlebars (besides for comments of course) generates some kind of output to the page, and they were designed to fit in your DOM unobtrusively, while still being visible. For clarity's sake, let's take a look at a very simple template:

```
<div>
    <h1>Hello {{name}}</h1>
</div>
```

> **Downloading the example code**
>
> You can download the example code files for all Packt books you have purchased from your account at http://www.PacktPub.com. If you purchased this book elsewhere, you can visit http://www.PacktPub.com/support and register to have the files e-mailed directly to you.

A template can consist of standard HTML (or plain text) and Handlebars tags. There are multiple kinds of tags as we will see throughout the course of the book, but the simplest ones are placeholders. All you do is wrap two pairs of curly braces around a placeholder key; this placeholder will be replaced with data when the template is processed.

This is much cleaner then the equivalent in PHP:

```
<h1>Hello <?= $name; ?></h1>
```

And definitely cleaner then entering the data with standard JavaScript:

```
elem.innerHTML = "<h1>Hello " + name + "</h1>";
```

This is just a single line; imagine doing the same thing with an entire page. Ultimately it's about using the right tool for the job, and Handlebars is definitely not the wrong tool.

So without any further delay let's jump straight into installation.

Installation

Handlebars is a template *engine* not a specific tool, so there are multiple ways you can use and install it. Handlebars templates can either be pre-compiled to improve performance, or you can compile them on the client side and have more flexibility with manipulating the templates themselves.

In this chapter we will take a look at downloading and setting up the necessary components to implement both of these methods.

Downloading the Handlebars library

Handlebars is easy to install as a js library since it has no other dependencies. To download the library, just go to `http://handlebarsjs.com/` and click on the big download button, this should take you to the script, which you can save on your computer as `handlebars.js`:

Installing this file is as simple as adding a script tag to your DOM with the path to this file:

```
<script src="handlebars.js"></script>
```

Precompiling templates

Compiling templates can be an expensive process. If you have a complex template, or even nested templates, it can slow down your production code. The solution to this is compiling the templates ahead of time. Then you will be left with pure JavaScript, which will make your overall page load much faster.

The first thing you will need to pre-compile your templates is node.js, which you can download and set up from `http://nodejs.org/download/`:

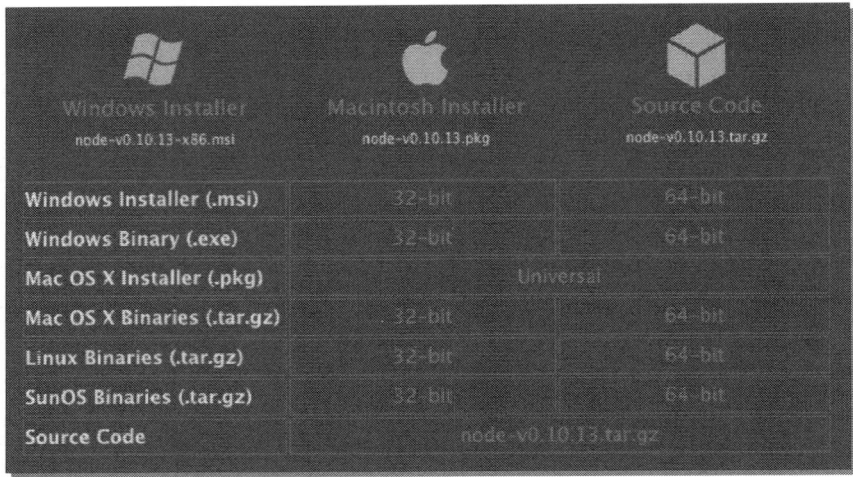

The setup wizard will install both node.js and the **node package manager** (**NPM**). With that ready, we can install the Handlebars CLI by running the following command in your terminal:

```
npm install -g handlebars
```

You don't have to worry too much about this if you are new to node.js. Basically this will download and place the Handlebars.js app into your path, so that you can use the `handlebars` command from your terminal.

Quick start – creating your first template

Let's start from the beginning. The purpose of using a templating engine such as Handlebars is to generate some kind of viewable content (usually HTML pages), dynamically. This encompasses a really broad range of uses, from e-mail newsletters, web apps, and really any other kind of output format around.

In this quick start, we will take a brief look at the process of creating a template with both placeholders and helper tags, and then how to run and output the contents to the page.

Preparing the project

To get started, create a file named `index.html` and add the following boilerplate code:

```html
<!DOCTYPE HTML>
<html>
  <head>
    <title>Handlebars Quickstart</title>
    <script src="handlebars.js"></script>
  </head>
  <body>
    <script>
      var src = "<h1>Hello {{name}}</h1>";
      var template = Handlebars.compile(src);

      var output = template({name: "Tom"});
      document.body.innerHTML += output;
    </script>
  </body>
</html>
```

This is a pretty good example to start with, as it demonstrates the minimum amount of code you will need to write to get a template on screen. We will start it by writing the template itself, just a pair of header tags with a greeting message inside. If you remember from the introduction, a Handlebars tag is a reference for some external data wrapped between two pairs of curly braces, and it signifies a dynamic point in the page where Handlebars will insert some information. Here we just want a property called "name" to be inserted at this point, which we will set in a moment. Once you have the template, the next step is where all the magic begins; Handlebars compile function will process through the template's source and generate a JavaScript function to output the result. What I mean by this is Handlebars will create a function that accepts some data and returns the final string with all the placeholders replaced.

An example of what I mean could be something like the following code for our quick template stated in the preceding paragraph:

```
var template = function (data) {
    return "<h1>Hello " + data.name + "</h1>";
}
```

And then every time the template gets called with data, the resulting string will be passed back. Now obviously it is a bit more complex than this, and Handlebars performs some escaping for you and other such checks, but the basic idea of what the compile function generates remains the same.

So with our template function created, we can call it by passing in some data (in this case the name Tom), and we take the output and append it to the body. After opening this page in a browser, you should see something like the following screenshot:

With the basics out of the way, let's take a look at helpers.

Block helpers

Helpers can be called in the same way as the data placeholder was called from the template. The difference between them is that a data placeholder will just take a static string or number and insert it into the template's output. Helpers on the other hand are functions, which first compute something, and then the results get placed into the output instead. You can think of helpers as a more dynamic form of placeholders.

Now there are two types of helpers in Handlebars: tag helpers, which work like regular functions; and block helpers, which have an added, nested template to manipulate.

Handlebars comes with a series of block helpers built-in, which allows you to perform basic logic in your templates. One of the most commonly used block helpers in Handlebars would have to be the each helper, which allows you to run a section of template per item in an array. Let's take a look at it in action.

It is going to be too messy to continue placing the templates into JavaScript strings like we did in the first example, so we will place it in its own script tag and pull it in. The reason we are using a script tag is because we don't want the template to show up on the page itself; by placing it in a script tag and setting the type to something the browser doesn't understand it will just be ignored. So right on top of the script tag block that we just wrote, add the following code:

```html
<script id="quickstart" type="template/handlebars">
  <h1>Hello {{name}}</h1>
  <ul>
    {{#each messages}}
      <li><b>{{from}}</b>: {{text}}</li>
    {{/each}}
  </ul>
</script>
```

We give the script tag an `id`, so we can access it later, and then we give it an arbitrary type, so that the browser doesn't try to parse it as JavaScript. Inside it we start with the same template code as before, and then we add each block to cycle through a list of messages and print out each one in a list element.

The next step is to replace the script block underneath with the new code, which will get the template from here:

```html
<script>
    var src = document.getElementById('quickstart').innerHTML;
    var template = Handlebars.compile(src);

  var output = template({
    name: "Tom",
    messages: [
      { from: "John", text: "Demo Message" },
      { from: "Bob", text: "Something Else" },
      { from: "John", text: "Second Post" }
    ]
  });
  document.body.innerHTML += output;
</script>
```

We start by pulling the template from the script block we added in the previous paragraph using standard JavaScript; next we compile it like before and run the template, this time with the added "`messages`" array. Running this in your browser will give you something like the following:

You may have picked up on this, but it's worth mentioning, that inside each block the context changes from the global data object passed into the template to the specific array element, because of this we are able to access its properties directly.

These first few steps have been simple, but subtly we have covered loading in templates from script tags, and the syntax for both standard placeholders as well as block helpers in your templates.

Top 6 features you need to know about

We just took a look at using both standard expressions and block helpers in your templates, but I think we are getting a little ahead of ourselves. Let's take a step back and talk about simple expressions.

Expressions

You already know that to output a simple JavaScript value, you simply wrap the properties key in two pairs of curly braces; but what you may not know is that forepart from just outputting the value, Handlebars is also HTML-encoding it. Take a look at the following code example:

```
<!DOCTYPE HTML>
<html>
  <head>
    <title>Handlebars Expressions</title>
    <script src="handlebars.js"></script>
  </head>
  <body>
    <script id="template" type="template/handlebars">
      {{content}}
    </script>
    <script>
      var src = document.getElementById("template").innerHTML;
      var template = Handlebars.compile(src);

      var output = template({content: "<h1>Hello</h1>"});
      document.body.innerHTML += output;
    </script>
  </body>
</html>
```

Running this in your browser will result in the following screenshot:

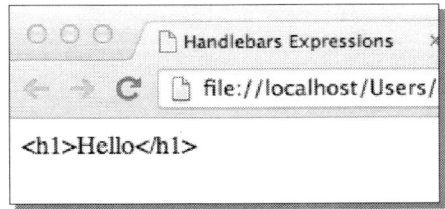

Instant Handlebars.js

The HTML is not being processed by the browser as it's being encoded beforehand. This is great for most uses, as for where you really want to insert only the content not the DOM itself; and in cases where you are handling user-submitted content, like comments for example, this is essential for keeping your UI and site from being altered.

With that being said, there are situations where you would want to insert DOM straight into the page without it being encoded. For example, if you are inserting a blog post, it may have DOM for headers and links and you wouldn't want the markup to show up on the page. Luckily, telling Handlebars to not encode something is as simple as adding a third pair of curly braces around the expression. In our previous example, change the word `{{content}}` to `{{{content}}}` and reload the page in your browser:

There really isn't much more that could be said about placeholders. You pass them into the template's function as we have been doing, and then you can output them either escaped or not, as we just saw. The next thing to discuss would be helpers.

Helpers

Handlebars comes with built-in helpers that we will get to, but I think it would be a lot more meaningful to see them once you know how they are built. So let's take a look at creating our first helper.

I have been saying that Handlebars has different kinds of helpers, but that is debatable. Internally there is only one "system" for helpers; but with that said, I think it helps conceptually to imagine two different types.

All helpers are essentially a function that returns a string, so for example, if you create a function that returns a capitalized version of a string, and registered it as a helper under the name `caps`, you would then be able to write in your templates and have Handlebars display your text (for example: `"hello world"`) capitalized in its place:

```
{{caps "hello world"}}
```

With that said, there are two ways to use a helper; in the *Quick start* section you saw the block form, where you prefix a hashtag to the helpers name and include more template code inside (we used the each helper), and here you saw how to use a function-styled helper.

So are they different kind of helpers or not? The truth of the matter is they are just two different "ways" of using the same helper. Every regular helper can be used as a block helper (although it wouldn't take advantage of the template code inside) and it is possible to create a helper that performs different actions depending on how it is used.

To register a new helper, you can simply use the "registerHelper" function on the Handlebars object. The function accepts two parameters:

- The name of the helper
- The function that will be called when the tag is used

An example to our `caps` helper could be something as follows:

```
Handlebars.registerHelper("caps", function(text) {
    return text.toUpperCase();
});
```

When you call a helper in Handlebars, all the parameters in the tags will be passed to this function, so you can essentially have as many as you want. Besides the parameters, there is one "system" variable that will be passed by Handlebars itself, but we are not using it here, so I have decided to leave it out of the function.

Inside, we are just converting the string to its uppercase form by using standard JS, and then returning it from the function.

Next, add a reference to our helper within the script tags, as in the following code example:

```
<!DOCTYPE HTML>
<html>
  <head>
    <title>Handlebars Helpers</title>
    <script src="handlebars.js"></script>
  </head>
  <body>
    <script id="template" type="template/handlebars">
      {{caps "hello"}}
    </script>
    <script>
      var src = document.getElementById("template").innerHTML;
      var template = Handlebars.compile(src);

      Handlebars.registerHelper("caps", function(text) {
        return text.toUpperCase();
      });

      var output = template();
```

```
        document.body.innerHTML += output;
      </script>
    </body>
</html>
```

Running this code in your browser, you should see the word "HELLO" being displayed prominently on your page.

This is a pretty simple example, showing some basic text manipulation, but you can pass anything to your functions (objects, numbers, Booleans, and so on), so the possibilities are pretty endless.

A common problem with the simple preceding example is that—as we mentioned earlier—double curly braces will escape any HTML code returned from the function. Let's say we create a helper that accepts an array of data and then outputs an HTML list with its information:

```
<!DOCTYPE HTML>
<html>
  <head>
    <title>Handlebars Helpers</title>
    <script src="handlebars.js"></script>
  </head>
  <body>
    <script id="template" type="template/handlebars">
      {{list numbers}}
    </script>
    <script>
      var src = document.getElementById("template").innerHTML;
      var template = Handlebars.compile(src);

      Handlebars.registerHelper("list", function(list) {
        var output = "<ul>";
        for (var i in list) {
          output += "<li>" + list[i] + "</li>";
        }
        output += "</ul>";
        return output;
      })
      var output = template({
        numbers: ["one", "two", "three", "four"]
      });
      document.body.innerHTML += output;
    </script>
  </body>
</html>
```

Try running this in your browser and you will get the following output:

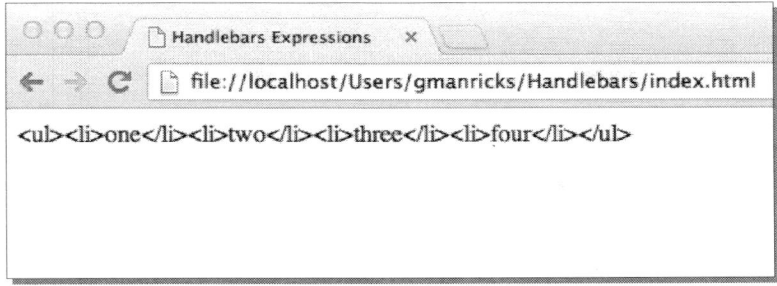

Not ideal. Sure you can use the triple curly brace style like we saw earlier, but there really is no point to this output, so for situations like this, Handlebars provides a type called `SafeString`, which basically tells Handlebars that it is already safe and no escaping is required.

This doesn't mean you shouldn't escape at all. If you are displaying user-defined data, then you definitely should escape that section, for safety's sake, if nothing else.

With both of these thoughts in mind, we are going to escape the individual array elements, which are coming from the outside; but we are going to return a `SafeString` variable, as the manual HTML we are adding internally should show up:

```
Handlebars.registerHelper("list", function(list) {
  var output = "<ul>";
  for (var i in list) {
  output += "<li>"
         + Handlebars.Utils.escapeExpression(list[i])
         + "</li>";
  }
  output += "</ul>";
return new Handlebars.SafeString(output);
});
```

Running this new version of the helper in your browser will now show the following:

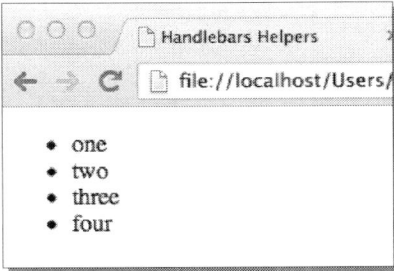

I mentioned earlier that apart from the regular parameters that are passed to your helpers, Handlebars adds a special system parameter to the end, which includes a couple of properties that you can use.

The first of those properties is the `hash` object; up until now we have been using the helper tags such as functions, and the order in which you specify the parameters is the order in which they will show up in the helper's function. But Handlebars also gives you the option of using attributes, just like in HTML tags. Let's modify our `caps` helper to also accept an attribute that will transform the text to lowercase instead:

```
Handlebars.registerHelper("caps", function(text, options){
  if (!options.hash.lower || options.hash.lower === "no") {
    return text.toUpperCase()
  } else {
    return text.toLowerCase()
  }
});
```

This time I am using the last parameter, and we are checking whether it's hash object is missing a key for `lower` or set to `"no"`. In both these cases, it will return the uppercase version of the string, otherwise it will return the lowercase object.

You can now try it out by using these in your template:

```
{{caps "Hello"}}
{{caps "Hello" lower="no"}}
{{caps "Hello" lower="yes"}}
```

You can use as many hash attributes as you want, but they should come after your regular parameters, as stated earlier.

Using these attributes you can create pretty powerful "vague" helpers and allow for a lot of configuration. The next property from the options parameter which could come in handy is the `data` attribute. This is very similar to the hash object, except that you pass it into the template function itself, so all the helpers will receive the same data.

This is great for global options that you want to set, and can be great for things such as multilanguage helpers or formatting dates, but also for setting global data such as the username for a profile page, which you may want to be available in all your helpers. Let's create a function that accepts a string and displays the correct version depending on the language:

```
Handlebars.registerHelper("greeting", function (options){
  switch (options.data.language) {
    case "en":
      return "Welcome"
    case "de":
      return "Willkommen"
```

```
    case "fr":
      return "Bienvenue"
    case "he":
      return "Baruch Haba"
    default:
      return "Welcome"
  }
})
```

This is pretty self-explanatory; we are going through a list of possible cases for the language data property. Next, we need to actually supply this property, which is done via the second option on the template call. Change your code at the bottom to this:

```
var output = template({}, {
data: {
    language: "en"
  }
});
```

The first object (the empty one) is the one we were using before and it sets the context variables and placeholders. The second is where you set system-level options specific to this template call. Here we are just setting the data attribute and giving it a property called language. The last step is to add the greeting tag to your template:

```
<script id="template" type="template/handlebars">
    {{greeting}}
</script>
```

Run this with different options for the language data property and you will see it is in fact working. Here we are simply using it in one place, but imagine building your entire site like this, you will then easily be able to render it to multiple demographics.

The last two properties that you can use on the options parameter are the fn and inverse properties. These are only available when using a helper in its block form, but essentially these are their embedded templates. If you remember what's going on, Handlebars converts your templates into regular JavaScript functions, which return the text back. In the case of a block helper, whatever is contained in the block gets converted into it's own function, and that function gets passed to a helper's function as the fn property. So what is the inverse for? Well, essentially the same thing.

Handlebars comes with a built-in tag called {{else}}, which can be used inside a block helper to signal a break: everything before it gets converted into a function for fn; and everything after the "else" (still inside the block) gets converted into a separate function and placed inside inverse.

Let's create our first block helper. What it will do is take a line-delimited list and convert it into an HTML select element:

```
1  {{#optionMe}}              1  <select>
2    yes                      2    <option value="yes">yes</option>
3    no            ─────▶     3    <option value="no">no</option>
4    maybe                    4    <option value="maybe">maybe</option>
5  {{/optionMe}}              5  </select>
```

The code for this is as follows:

```
Handlebars.registerHelper("optionMe", function(options){
  var list = options.fn();
  list = list.trim().split("\n");

  var out = "<select>";
  for (var i in list) {
    var item = list[i].trim();
    out += "<option value='" + item + "'>"
         + item
         + "</option>";
  }
  out += "</select>";
  return out;
});
```

It is a fairly simple example; the only new part is the bit at the beginning where we use the `fn` function. Since the contained template code has already been converted to a function, we can use it like any other JavaScript function that returns a string. So we pull in the contents, split it by newline, and cycle through the array, to create the final HTML select element. It is worth mentioning that you don't need to return a safe string, as Handlebars doesn't try to escape it. This is due to the fact that `options.fn` is already being escaped automatically, and if it escapes the outer helper as well, your content will be double-escaped.

To use this, change your template to the following:

```
<script id="template" type="template/handlebars">
  {{#optionMe}}
    dog
    cat
    turtle
    rabbit
    horse
  {{/optionMe}}
</script>
```

Then run the page in your browser, and if all went well, you should see the following screenshot as a result:

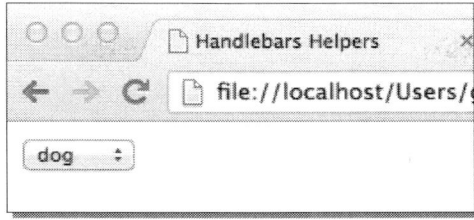

This example illustrates the use of the `fn` function, but what it holds is more than just the text between the helper tags; the `fn` function is in itself like the main call to the template. This means you can pass it context information and other properties and manipulate its output that way.

For example's sake, let's create a block helper that accepts a number and creates its list of exponents:

```
Handlebars.registerHelper("listX", function (number, options) {
  var num = parseInt(number);
  var out = "";

  for (var i = 1; i <= 10; i++) {
    var data = {
      number: i,
      result: Math.pow(num, i)
    }
    out += options.fn(data);
  }

  return out;
});
```

The function starts by parsing the input, which could be a string, and converts it into an `int`. We then loop `i` from 1 to 10, compute the data, and pass it to the `options.fn` template. Finally, we combine the results from the different iterations and return the resulting string.

As you can see from this helper, we have access to the following two placeholders that we can use freely:

- `number`: The current exponent
- `result`: The result from the calculation

Instant Handlebars.js

So let's use these two placeholders (you don't need to use them all, but I will). Add the following to your template:

```
<ul>
  {{#listX 8}}
    <li><b>8<sup>{{number}}</sup></b> = {{result}}</li>
  {{/listX}}
</ul>
```

In essence this template is saying, "give me the first 10 exponents for the number 8, and format the results in the following HTML." Running this in your browser should produce the following screenshot:

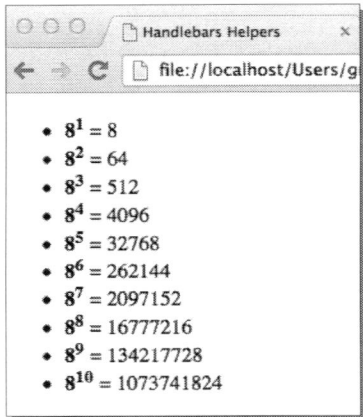

With that, I hope you see the difference between tag helpers and block helpers, A block helper computes some information, or modifies the template's context, but ultimately it can let you choose how to display the information. Regular helpers on the other hand are for situations where you have a predefined format that you always want the results to be in, and they allow you to segment these components out into simple privatized tags.

I would now like to discuss the `inverse` property on the `options` variable; I have gone through it in passing but let's take a look at using it in action. The way it works is that you place a `{{else}}` tag inside your block helper and everything after it will be converted into a separate template function and stored inside `inverse`. To demonstrate this, let's build a helper which will accept a list of notifications, and if the notification is flagged as important, then it will use the `inverse` template, otherwise it will render the notification with the regular `fn` function:

```
Handlebars.registerHelper("notifications", function(notifs, options){
  var out = "";
  for (var i in notifs) {
    if (notifs[i].important) {
      out += options.inverse(notifs[i]);
    } else {
```

```
      out += options.fn(notifs[i]);
    }
  }
  return out;
});
```

The function cycles through the list of notifications and checks the important property, as I said earlier, and it then takes the results from the different template calls and returns it. The next thing we need is to create a list of notifications that contain an important field and whatever else we may want to use:

```
var notifications = [
  { title: "process #235 finished running", important: false },
  { title: "assets have been compiled", important: false },
  { title: "web server has crashed !!", important: true },
  { title: "22 unread emails in inbox", important: false },
  { title: "worker #3444 waiting for input", important: true }
];
var output = template({notes: notifications});
```

These may not be the most creative notifications, but they will serve our purpose. You can see at the bottom that we have to remember to pass them to the template call so that we can have access to them. The last step is to actually create the template itself:

```
<script id="template" type="template/handlebars">
  {{#notifications notes}}
    <div>{{title}}</div>
  {{else}}
    <div style="color:red">
      <b>{{title}}</b>
    </div>
  {{/notifications}}
</script>
```

Essentially, we are writing to different templates, each for a separate situation: the top is the normal layout; and the second (after the "else") is for special cases, which for us is the more important notifications. Running this in your browser should produce the following screenshot as output:

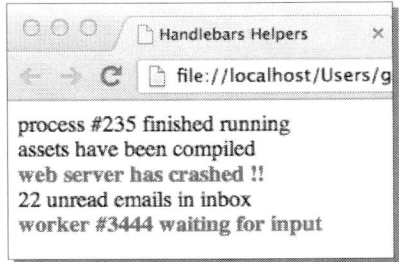

Instant Handlebars.js

With all the different components discussed, let's build another Handlebars helper, but this time one that can be used as both a normal tag helper as well as a block helper. For lack of a better idea, and due to the fact that I don't want to pull in any third-party libraries yet, let's build a helper which will convert an object filled with data into a form for editing.

The way it will work is that it will check the type of each property and generate the appropriate input type (text input for strings, checkboxes for Booleans, and so on); finally wrapping it with form tags and adding a submit button. If you use this helper as a tag helper, it will just list the properties in order, whereas if you use it as a block helper, it will just compute the HTML and let you arrange it the way you like. For the sake of clarity, I will show you the entire helper first, and then we will go through it piece by piece:

```
Handlebars.registerHelper("formIt", function(data, options){
var fields = {};
  //Generate the Inputs
  for (var k in data) {
    var v = data[k];
    var html = "";
    switch (typeof v) {
      case "string":
        v = Handlebars.Utils.escapeExpression(v);
        html = '<input type="text" name="'
            + k + '" value="' + v + '" />';
        break;
      case "number":
        html = '<input type="number" name="'
            + k + '" value="' + v + '" />';
        break;
      case "boolean":
        var checked = (v) ? "checked" : "";
        html = '<input type="checkbox" name="'
            + k + '" ' + checked + ' />';
        break;
    }
    fields[k] = new Handlebars.SafeString(html);
  }

  var out = "<form>";

  if (typeof options.fn == "undefined") {
    //If it's a tag helper then add each element manually
    for (var k in fields) {
      out += "<div>" + k + ": " + fields[k] + "</div>";
    }
    //Add the button
```

```
      out += '<input type="submit" value="submit">';
    } else {
      //If it's a block helper add the button and run the template
      var button = '<input type="submit" value="submit">';
      fields.submit = new Handlebars.SafeString(button);
      out += options.fn(fields);
    }

    out += "</form>";
    return new Handlebars.SafeString(out);
  });
```

It's pretty long, but let's walk through it; the first loop will cycle through the passed-in data and for each field will create an HTML input element. We are doing this with a switch statement based on the type of the properties value. In this example I am using a text input for strings, a number input for numbers, and a checkbox for Booleans. Since this could be potentially used with user data, I am escaping the strings to be safe, but the numbers and Booleans are intrinsically safe, so they can be used directly. After each input is computed, we store it in the fields object, making sure to preserve the properties name.

The second step is to check whether this is a tag helper or block helper. This can be achieved easily enough by simply checking if the `fn` property on options is defined.

The first case we are covering is the tag helper. Here we just want to cycle through each field, display it's name, and then append the HTML input. With all the fields concatenated, we add the submit button and we are good to go.

The second situation (the "else") is for when we are dealing with a block helper. Here we want the user to be able to place the inputs however they want, so we simply add the button to the fields list and then run the entire object through the `fn` template. Finally, to finish things off we create a new safe string and return the output.

It's long but I wouldn't say it's complicated. To use this helper, I am going to create a really simple object to represent a user:

```
var userData = {
  name: "John Smith",
  age: 25,
  newsletter: true
};

var output = template({user: userData});
```

Instant Handlebars.js

Basically one property for each type, just to test it out; next let's set the template:

```
<script id="template" type="template/handlebars">
  <div>
    <h2>Block Version</h2>
    {{#formIt user}}
      <div>Name: {{name}}</div>
      <div>Age: {{age}}</div>
      <div>Receive Newsletter ?: {{newsletter}}</div>
      {{submit}}
    {{/formIt}}
  </div>
  <div>
    <h2>Tag Version</h2>
    {{formIt user}}
  </div>
</script>
```

In this template we are using the helper in both its block form as well as its tag form. The block form requires more code but allows for more customization; it's a trade-off, and providing both options is always nice.

After running this page in your browser, it will give you something that looks like the following screenshot:

Now give yourself a pat on the back, because you've just learned pretty much everything there is to know about creating helpers in Handlebars. With this new-found knowledge, it makes sense to now go through the built-in helpers and see how they were put together.

The first helper we should take a look at is the `if` block helper:

```
Handlebars.registerHelper('if', function(conditional, options) {
  var type = toString.call(conditional);
  if (type === functionType) {
    conditional = conditional.call(this);
  }

  if (!conditional || Handlebars.Utils.isEmpty(conditional)) {
    return options.inverse(this);
  } else {
    return options.fn(this);
  }
});
```

This helper accepts one parameter, which is the variable to test. The first four lines check whether the passed-in parameter is a function, because if it is we want to test its results, not its presence.

Next we check if the variable has a `false` value. This is accomplished using a built-in utility called `isEmpty`, which looks like this:

```
function isEmpty (value) {
  if (!value && value !== 0) {
    return true;
  } else if (toString.call(value) === "[object Array]"
          && value.length === 0) {
    return true;
  } else {
    return false;
  }
}
```

This small function just checks two different "empty" states: the first is whether the value evaluates to false but does not equal zero. Zero is a valid number, and so just because the variable has the number zero, does not mean it's empty. What this will catch though is things like empty strings, as they evaluate to false but not zero.

The second state we look for is whether the object is an array but has no elements inside, as that is an empty variable. If either of these situations are true, the function will return true; otherwise it returns false, as the variable is not empty.

Back to our `if` helper. You can now see that what we are saying is: if the value is empty or zero (because of the added `!conditional`), we will return the inverse block (the template after the `{{else}}`), otherwise we return the regular block template.

The next helper I want to take a look at is the `unless` helper. The `unless` helper is the exact opposite of the `if` helper; so if the value is false the regular template will be called. This was a cool helper to look at, and I was pleasantly surprised in how it was implemented:

```
Handlebars.registerHelper('unless', function(conditional, options) {
  return Handlebars.helpers['if'].call(
    this,
    conditional,
    {fn: options.inverse, inverse: options.fn}
  );
});
```

If you didn't catch it right away, then what it is doing is calling the `if` block helper, but swapping the `fn` with the `inverse` function, and vice versa. It's a clever trick, which both reuses code and, more importantly, keeps this function an exact opposite to its counterpart. If we were dealing solely with Booleans we would have been able to just reverse the conditional variable, but if you remember, it can really contain anything, even a function, so this output swap simplifies the need to test types and outputs.

The next helper is called `with` and allows you to change the context on the template inside it. Here is the entire function:

```
Handlebars.registerHelper('with', function(context, options) {
  var type = toString.call(context);
  if(type === functionType) {
    context = context.call(this);
  }

  if (!Handlebars.Utils.isEmpty(context))
    return options.fn(context);
});
```

It accepts one parameter that is the new context; which could be a function like before, in which case it will be processed. Finally, assuming the context isn't empty, we run the block helpers template, setting our variable as the context.

The last real helper I want to go through now is the `each` helper. This is the longest helper by far, mostly because it was written as vague as possible to work with multiple variable types:

```
Handlebars.registerHelper('each', function(context, options) {
  var fn = options.fn, inverse = options.inverse;
  var i = 0, ret = "", data;
```

```
    var type = toString.call(context);
    if (type === functionType) {
      context = context.call(this);
    }

    if (options.data) {
      data = Handlebars.createFrame(options.data);
    }

    if (context && typeof context === 'object') {
      if (context instanceof Array) {
        for (var j = context.length; i<j; i++) {
          if (data) {
            data.index = i;
          }
          ret = ret + fn(context[i], { data: data });
        }
      } else {
        for (var key in context) {
          if (context.hasOwnProperty(key)) {
            if (data) {
              data.key = key;
            }
            ret = ret + fn(context[key], {data: data});
            i++;
          }
        }
      }
    }

    if (i === 0) {
      ret = inverse(this);
    }

    return ret;
});
```

Let's go through this line by line. The first two lines just set some initial variables:

- `fn/inverse`: It separates this out for convenience
- `i`: A variable to hold the number of iterations that have been executed
- `ret`: The string this function will return
- `data`: An object that will be used to clone the global data (more on this in a minute)

Next we check whether the past in context is a function, just like in the other, so that we can work with its output instead of the function itself. After that we have an `if` statement which populates the data object: this `Handlebars.createFrame` function is essentially cloning the global data object passed into the template for local use. Because of how JavaScript objects are implemented, if you pass an object to a function it won't create a copy, rather it passes the original, so any changes will propagate outside the function, which isn't what we want.

As of JavaScript 1.8.5, you can clone an object using `Object.create`, but just in case you don't have this function available, Handlebars implements it for older browsers, which is what the `createFrame` function is for.

With the data object ready and our context sorted out, the next `if` statement makes sure we are dealing with an object. In JavaScript, both Arrays and Objects have a type of "object," so we check to make sure that we are dealing with either of these. Next we have two blocks that are essentially the same: just one handles the event where the context is an array; and one handles the case where it is an object. You can see that on every iteration we are incrementing `i`.

The other thing you may be wondering is why we are setting the index or key into the data object for each template. The answer to this is quite simple. I haven't mentioned this yet because it's better to use the regular context object, but you have full access to all properties in the data object, simply by pre-pending an `@` symbol to the beginning of its key. In this case, let's say you ran an `each` statement on an object, you can access the current key by typing `{{@key}}`, and the same would be true for the index in the case of an array.

The last `if` statement is just checking whether `i` equals 0. If you have been keeping track, if `i` equals 0, it means no iterations have been performed; in other words the object/array was empty. If that is the case, it runs the `inverse` template passing through `this`, which contains the current context.

forepart from these built-in helpers, Handlebars supplies one wildcard helper, for when you use a helper that doesn't exist. It attempts to do something meaningful with the name that was given, and in most cases does a good job at that. Let's take a look:

```
Handlebars.registerHelper('blockHelperMissing', function(context,
options) {
  var inverse = options.inverse || function() {},
    fn = options.fn;

  var type = toString.call(context);

  if (type === functionType) {
    context = context.call(this);
  }

  if (context === true) {
    return fn(this);
```

```
      } else if (context === false || context == null) {
        return inverse(this);
      } else if(type === "[object Array]") {
        if(context.length > 0) {
          return Handlebars.helpers.each(context, options);
        } else {
          return inverse(this);
        }
      } else {
        return fn(context);
      }
    });
```

This helper gets called with the data from your context array. So, say you call a block helper like `{{#users}}` and you have an array named users in your context, that array will be passed to this helper as the first parameter.

Again, as before, it stores references to both `fn` and `inverse` locally, just for convenience's sake, and checks whether the context is a function as you have come to expect. The next thing it does is try to do something meaningful depending on the variables type. If we are dealing with a Boolean, it will test the Boolean and run the `fn`/`inverse`, as though you had used it with the `{{#if}}` block helper.

If we are dealing with an array, it will run it as though you used an `each` helper, by looping through each element; or if the array is empty, it will run the inverse template. Last, but not least, if it doesn't match any of the above, for example a string or an object, it will run it as though you had used the `{{#with}}` helper.

This single helper allows you to shorthand all the other block helpers, provided you use the right variable type, and I think it illustrates well the concepts of abstractions, and code reuse well.

We are now completely done with helpers, so the next topic I would like to cover is partials.

> You can read the docs on block helpers at: `http://handlebarsjs.com/block_helpers.html`.

Partials

Partials, as its title denotes, is a system for creating "widgets" or sections of templates that can be used and reused throughout all of your templates. You can see this being used a lot for example with the nav bar when building a website. It is generally the same code, and instead of adding it to every page manually, you simply create a partial with its code and plug it in.

So what's the difference between a helper and a partial? A helper is a function, a block of code, which computes some value and returns some text to be placed. A partial on the other hand is more like a snippet; it's a piece of template code, which will literally be inserted wherever you call it. It doesn't compute anything on its own; its contents get implanted into the rest of your template and then processed along with it. There isn't one that is better then the other, they are for different things completely, and when we get to project organization, you will see they allow you to separate code into pieces that make sense without compromising on functionality.

So let's build our first partial, I am going to create a new HTML file for this to keep things neat:

```html
<!DOCTYPE HTML>
<html>
  <head>
    <title>Handlebars Helpers</title>
    <script src="handlebars.js"></script>
  </head>
  <body>

    <script id="template" type="template/handlebars">
      <h1>My Site</h1>
      {{> greetings}}
    </script>

    <script>
      var partialSrc = "Hello {{name}}";
      Handlebars.registerPartial("greetings", partialSrc);

      var templateSrc = document.getElementById("template")
                        .innerHTML;
      var template = Handlebars.compile(templateSrc);

      var data = {
        name: "Gabriel"
      }

      document.body.innerHTML += template(data);
    </script>
  </body>
</html>
```

This is essentially the same setup as we had in the last file, so I am not going to go through the file itself; but let's take a look at the template. The first line is standard HTML, but on the second line we have a new tag that is the partial tag. Internally, Handlebars has a couple of different systems for handling partials, depending on whether they are included, compiled, or even pre-computed; but no matter how it is called, it is best to think of a partial as though it is going to be inserted directly where the partial tag is placed. This means the context is the same, and any settings from encompassing helpers are available to your partial.

In the second script tag you can see that to register a partial, we simply call the `registerPartial` function on the Handlebars object, passing in a name and the source for the partial. You can pass in a pre-compiled template function instead of the source, but we will get to that soon.

Everything else is exactly like what we are used too. We added the name property to the template, and, like I said, the partial receives the same context as the template, so it will have access to it as well. Running this in your browser should produce a result similar to the following screenshot:

With our current setup it is a bit difficult to see how this drastically benefits us. So let's set up our files, assuming that you would be working on a large site; because once you are working with multiple files and reusing code, partials become essential.

Structuring a Handlebars app
When working on projects, which contain a lot of frontend JavaScript, it becomes essential to modularize your code, and because of this, libraries like RequireJS were built. So let's take a moment and familiarize ourselves with RequireJS and AMD in general.

Having an application with many JS scripts introduces a couple of issues: first, you need to add them all to your files, which means each HTML document will contain 10–15 script tags to loading in, and is messy; second, sending a request to fetch an external script takes time, which is one of the slowest processes when loading a page and bottlenecks your site's load times. Finally, having multiple separate `js` files makes it hard to manage dependencies; some files may need to load before others, and arranging them in your documents can become tedious.

Introducing **AMD** (**Asynchronous Module Definition**); what this is, is a style of structuring your app into modules. ach module expresses its dependencies and is self-contained, so you don't need to worry about namespace issues. Then you have one loader script which will pull these resources when and only when they are needed, making sure that you don't load unnecessary code, slowing load time. This allows for quicker/neater apps that are easier to manage.

RequireJS is an implementation of such a loader, and it contains a lot of options for loading in different kinds of resources, as we will soon see. So let's get started creating a new app.

Inside a new folder, create an `index.html` file, and then create a `js` folder to keep our scripts. Inside the `js` folder, create a folder named `helpers`, a folder named `partials`, and a folder named `templates`. Last, but not least, we will need to place the `handlebars.js` file we have been using into this `js` folder, and we will need to download `require.js` and the `text.js` files. These can both be found at `http://requirejs.org/docs/download.html`. Your final structure should look like the following screenshot:

```
├── index.html
└── js
    ├── handlebars.js
    ├── helpers
    ├── partials
    ├── require.js
    ├── templates
    └── text.js

4 directories, 4 files
```

Now open up your `index.html` file and let's set it up:

```
<!DOCTYPE HTML>
<html>
<head>
  <meta charset="utf-8">
  <title>Handlebars AMD</title>
</head>
<body>

  <script src="js/require.js" type="text/javascript" data-main="js/main"></script>
</body>
</html>
```

If this is your first time using something like `require.js`, then you may be surprised to see how empty this file actually is; we have a single line to include `require.js`. Then you may notice that we have attached a property called `data-main` and set it to a file named `main` in the `js` folder.

Now don't worry if you are a bit lost, it's to be expected if this is your first time using `require.js`, but don't worry, it is very simple in nature, and after this example you will have a good grasp on how to use it for yourself.

The `script` tag is doing two separate things: first of all we are loading the `require.js` file itself, as one would expect; but second, by setting the `data-main` option, we are telling `require.js` to immediately load the given file and run it on launch.

In `require.js` you will see that you can generally leave the extension off `js` files, and it will add it internally, so this call to `js/main` is really referring to `js/main.js`. To verify that this is in fact working, create a file named `main.js` inside the `js` folder and simply add a line like `console.log("loaded");`, so we are assured that it's being run.

Due to a security precaution, your browser `require.js` won't actually be able to load local files, so you will need to run this from a web server. You may be using something such as MAMP or WAMP already, which will work fine, but if you have PHP 5.4 or versions later than this installed on your system, then you can simply run the following from a terminal window, which is navigated to the `project` directory to boot up a temporary server for our purposes:

```
php -S localhost:8888
```

Either way, once you have a server running and the `main.js` file created, navigate to the `index` file in your browser, and you should see the following in your terminal:

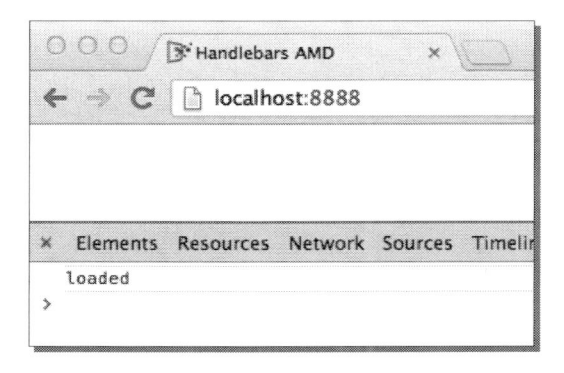

If you see the word "loaded" in the console, then you are good to go: RequireJS is installed. Now the next step is to set up Handlebars.

This can be accomplished in a number of ways, each having its own pros and cons; so we are going to go through 2–3 different arrangements, trading off complexity for flexibility.

I want to actually start off with a more complex setup, as it closer matches what we have been doing, and I think it's a great introduction to using RequireJS with Handlebars.

One problem you will find with `require.js`, or really any AMD system, is the fact that JavaScript doesn't have access to the file system. So you can't just say "load all files from the `helpers` folder," as it has no way of accessing the folder to see what's inside. If you were using server-side JS like node.js, then you would be able to do something like this, but in the browser we have to manually specify each one.

To keep our actual modules clean, let's create some code to pre-compute an array with all the files and their paths. Add the following to your `main.js`:

```
var helpers = [];
var partials = [];
var deps = [];
for (var i in helpers) {
  deps.push('h/' + helpers[i]);
}

for (var i in partials) {
  deps.push('text!p/' + partials[i] + ".partial");
}
```

If you remember, helpers are JavaScript but partials are just plain text, so the first to loop just takes the names of the helpers from the first array and adds their path to the `deps` array. The second to loop, though, adds a prefix of `text!` and has to specify a file extension as well as the name, as these are not `js` files. In RequireJS, when you have a word followed by an exclamation mark, it denotes a plugin: in our case it's the `text.js` plugin we downloaded earlier.

Standard AMD is for loading JavaScript modules, not for loading plain text files; this plugin allows you to load regular text files as variables, which for partials is perfect.

You may also have noticed I didn't specify the path to the `helpers` or `partials` directory, instead I just wrote h or p; this is a personal preference, as RequireJS allows you to create substitution paths, so that every time it get a path to h we can have it convert that to `helpers`. This is not required and you can leave it out if you want to, by simply writing out the full path (`helpers` and `partials`). With our files ready, we need to configure `require.js` itself:

```
require.config({
  paths: {
    "t": "templates",
    "p": "partials",
    "h": "helpers"
  },
```

```
      shim: {
        "handlebars": {
          "exports": "Handlebars",
          "deps": deps
        }
      },
      config: {
        "H": {
          "helpers": helpers,
          "partials": partials
        }
      }
    });
```

There are a number of things going on here so I will walk you through it. The first `paths` property is the substitutions array I just spoke about. The next property named `shim` is for converting non-AMD-compliant modules for use in your `require.js` app. The Handlebars library was not written as an AMD module, so what this definition is saying is "create a module named "Handlebars" loaded from the same file, and export the Handlebars variable." As you will see in a second, modules are self-contained and just return a single value, which is how you interface with it. When you shim a library, it is usually declared globally, so this line tells RequireJS to return the global "Handlebars" variable when this submodule is loaded.

The last setting here just sets the dependencies, which, if you have been following, you will know contains the links to all the helpers and partials. These aren't really dependencies to Handlebars, but we want them loaded at the same time.

Last, but not least, we have the `config` property. This allows you to assign properties to modules, which they will be able to access locally. What this property is doing is assigning the helpers and partials as settings on a module named "H." What's "H"? Well it's a module we are about to create.

We did just create a shim for Handlebars, but we don't want that version of Handlebars to be used, because it's missing all the helpers and partials. So we are going to create our own module named `H`, which will load all the partials and helpers, register them, and return the fully loaded copy of Handlebars, so it will be ready for use.

To build this module, create a new file named `H.js` inside the `js` folder and add the following:

```
    define(['handlebars', 'module', 'require'],
              function (H, module, require) {

    });
```

This is what a module looks like; you begin by specifying a list of dependencies, and then, once those are loaded, it will call the attached function, passing in each dependency as a variable. Whatever this function returns is what gets exported to any other code that loads this module.

We aren't really creating any new logic; rather we are building a "pass-through" module, which is a programing concept of intercepting a variable and modifying it, similar to a middleware paradigm.

The first dependency is the Handlebars shim we just set up, and it will contain the Handlebars variable. The next dependency is the "module" module: this is provided by RequireJS itself and allows us to access the `config` setting that we assigned to this module in `main.js`. The last dependency is `require.js` itself, as we will be pulling in the individual helpers and partials.

It is worth noting that this kind of dynamic requires statements and is only possible because we already loaded these files as a dependency to Handlebars, if you remember, in `main.js`; otherwise the dependencies wouldn't be ready and the function would return before the async modules could be loaded, causing an error.

Anyway, inside this function we will pull the list of helpers and partials from the options we set, and one by one, register them into Handlebars, and finally return the fully loaded Handlebars variable for use by other modules:

```
define(
    ['handlebars', 'module', 'require'],
    function (H, module, require) {

    var opts = module.config();

    for (var i in opts.helpers) {
      var helper = opts.helpers[i];
      var func = require('h/' + helper);
      H.registerHelper(helper, func);
    }

    for (var i in opts.partials) {
      var partial = opts.partials[i];
      var src = require('text!p/' + partial + ".partial");
      H.registerPartial(partial, src);
    }

    return H;
}
);
```

I don't think this code requires any further information, as it does exactly what I just said it would.

The next step would be to test everything. Let's create a file named `home.template` inside the `templates` directory that contains the following code:

```
{{> header}}
  Welcome back {{userfy name}}!
{{> footer}}
```

This code calls two partials, one named header and one named footer, and between them we call a helper named `userfy`, which will convert a standard name into a username format. This isn't a really useful or realistic helper, but it will illustrate the concepts as well as test out our system.

Let's now create these partials. Create a file named `header.partial` inside the `partials` folder that contains:

```
<h1>Our Site's Header</h1>
```

And then another partial named `footer.partial` that contains:

```
<p><b>&copy; Our Site</b> - This is the Footer</p>
```

Next we need to create the helper, a regular AMD module. So create a file called `userfy.js` inside the `helpers` directory with the following code:

```
define([], function(){
  return function(name) {
    var username = name.toLowerCase().replace(/ /g, "_");
    return username;
  }
});
```

It's written just like the "H" module we wrote, except it has no dependencies, so we can just leave the array blank, and then it returns the helpers function. The helper just converts the name to lowercase and then replaces all spaces to underscores.

Now go back to the `main.js` file and add these new files to the appropriate arrays at the top:

```
var helpers = [
  "userfy"
];

var partials = [
  "header",
  "footer"
];
```

Last, but not least, we need to "glue" all the pieces together, by adding the following to the bottom of `main.js`:

```
require(['H', 'text!t/home.template'], function(H, src) {
  var template = H.compile(src);

  var context = {
    name: "John Smith"
  };

  document.body.innerHTML += template(context);
});
```

It has a similar structure to a module definition, except that it isn't meant to return anything; instead you just load in other modules for use. Here we are loading in our custom Handlebars module along with the home template we wrote. Inside the function, we compile it down, assign the data, and append the results to the page. Running this in your browser should display the following result:

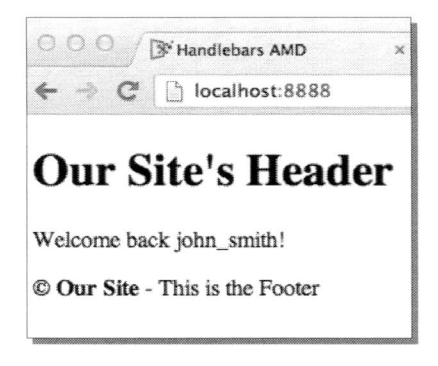

Our Site's Header

Welcome back john_smith!

© Our Site - This is the Footer

With this structure, all the templates remain in plain text, which allows you to modify them on the client, and even create meta templates after the fact. But, as you just saw, it did require a bit of hackery to load everything in, as we needed to set the partials and helpers as dependencies on the Handlebars shim, plus the browser still had to load all our files. With that said, this is probably the best setup for prototyping as well as local development, but when you are ready to deploy, there are more efficient setups.

Precompilation

In the setup chapter we installed the Handlebars app using node.js. That app allows you to pre-compile the different templates and partials into standard JavaScript, and it even has an option to output AMD modules, which we can use directly with `require.js`.

Let's compile a sample template to get a better idea of what I mean. Open a terminal window and navigate to the folder where our app is. If you are uncomfortable with the terminal this can be achieved by typing "cd", and then dragging the folder onto the terminal window. For me, the folder's path is `~/Handlebars/AMD`, so the command will end up being:

cd ~/Handlebars/AMD

Once inside the directory, let's create a new `template` named `demo.template` and fill it with the following:

```
Hello {{world}}
```

You can create the file and populate it in the terminal using:

```
echo "Hello {{world}}" > templates/demo.template
```

We aren't going to actually use this template in our app, but let's compile it just to see what the output looks like. In the terminal window, enter the following to compile the template:

```
handlebars templates/demo.template
```

The output should look like this:

```
(function() {
    var template = Handlebars.template, templates =
      Handlebars.templates = Handlebars.templates || {};
    return templates['demo.template'] = template(function
      (Handlebars,depth0,helpers,partials,data) {

    this.compilerInfo = [4,'>= 1.0.0'];
    helpers = this.merge(helpers, Handlebars.helpers); data =
      data || {};
    var buffer = "", stack1, functionType="function",
      escapeExpression=this.escapeExpression;

  buffer += "Hello ";
  if (stack1 = helpers.world) {
    stack1 = stack1.call(depth0, {hash:{},data:data});
  } else {
    stack1 = depth0.world;
      stack1 = typeof stack1 === functionType ?
        stack1.apply(depth0) : stack1;
  }
      buffer += escapeExpression(stack1) + "\n";
  return buffer;
  });
})();
```

Instant Handlebars.js

If you are new to JavaScript, then the structure of the code is a self-invoking function, and the reason for doing this is to keep it contained and prevent it from messing with local/global variables. The first block of code before the empty line just initializes some variables and pulls in some Handlebars properties, then it starts by adding the word `Hello` to a buffer variable, as this is plain text in the template, it knows it will never be changed. The rest of the function is added because of the reference to `{{world}}`. It checks if there is a helper named `world`, in which case it will call it, otherwise it takes "world" from the context variable. Once the placeholder has been computed, it escapes it before finally returning the entire buffer.

This code may not be the most clean or readable code, but it's not meant to be. This code was generated via the Handlebars algorithm and is not meant to be modified manually; to edit things you should modify the template and regenerate the code.

Next, let's add the `-a` flag to make it output an AMD module:

```
handlebars -a templates/demo.template
```

You can see the template is pretty much the same except that it is now wrapped in a module format and has Handlebars set as a dependency:

```
define(['handlebars'], function(Handlebars) {
    var template = Handlebars.template, templates =
      Handlebars.templates = Handlebars.templates || {};

    return templates['demo.template'] = template(function
      (Handlebars,depth0,helpers,partials,data) {

        this.compilerInfo = [4,'>= 1.0.0'];
        helpers = this.merge(helpers, Handlebars.helpers); data =
          data || {};

    var buffer = "", stack1, functionType="function",
      escapeExpression=this.escapeExpression;

      buffer += "Hello ";
      if (stack1 = helpers.world) {
        stack1 = stack1.call(depth0, {hash:{},data:data});
      } else {
        stack1 = depth0.world;
        stack1 = typeof stack1 === functionType ?
          stack1.apply(depth0) : stack1;
      }
        buffer += escapeExpression(stack1) + "\n";
      return buffer;
    });
});
```

In our current setup, we have a pass-through module, which we use to load everything in. In our new setup, everything is AMD-compliant and no compiling is required, so we don't need to have the H module. I am not going to erase any of the other files, because as I said, it is better for development; so an easy way to keep both is to create a new file named production.js inside the js folder, where we will keep the production code. Also, create a folder named precomp, where we will place all the pre-compiled contents.

Let's start production.js with an initial setup:

```
require.config({
  paths: {
    "p": "precomp",
    "h": "helpers"
  },
  shim: {
    "handlebars": {
      "exports": "Handlebars"
    }
  }
});
```

It's much shorter than before because we don't need to specify dependencies or configure any modules. In the paths, I specified both the precomp folder as well as the helpers folder, as we still need access to the helpers.

Next, let's compile down our files. Let's begin with the home template: run this command in your terminal:

**handlebars -a -e template -f precomp/home.js \
templates/home.template**

The -a tag we saw before tells the compiler to output an AMD module. Next, we set the input files extension: we are using .template files, so you can simply set this to template. We need to set this option otherwise the template will be compiled under the name home.template instead of just home. It isn't such a big deal in our case since we are only using one template and we will be calling it directly, but if we were using multiple templates, it could be an issue.

The next step is to compile the partials, we aren't going to compile one at a time, as then it would need to load each; it is a lot more efficient to just group them together. You can do this for the templates too, but since you only ever load one at a time, it seems beneficial to compile them separately.

The command to compile down the partials is:

**handlebars -a -p -e partial -f precomp/partials.js \
partials/**

It is very similar to the previous command except we added the `-p` tag to tell it we are dealing with partials and not templates. The extension is also set to `.partial`, and instead of specifying just one partial file, we are loading all of them just by specifying the directory.

We now have access to these, so let's write our code inside of the `production.js` file to render our page:

```
require(
  ['p/home', 'h/userfy', 'p/partials'],
  function (home, userfy, partials) {

  var helpers = {
    "userfy": userfy
  };

  var html = home({name: "Gabriel"}, {helpers: helpers});

  document.body.innerHTML += html;
});
```

We don't need to load Handlebars itself as the individual modules will load it already. Also you may have noticed that all the extensions can be left off since we are only using `js` files.

Another thing worth mentioning is the fact that the partials already register themselves into Handlebars, so we don't need to do anything with them, just include them, but the helpers on the other hand just return a function, so we need to add it to the template when we call it.

The last step to get this running is to change the main script inside the `index.html` file from `main` to `production`. The completed line should look like the following:

```
<script src="js/require.js" type="text/javascript" data-
  main="js/production"></script>
```

This way you can still use the other option when prototyping and testing, but once you have the list of helpers and partials you will be using, and have the final version of the template, you can compile everything and switch the version for production.

Running the code in your browser again should produce the following screenshot as output:

Our Site's Header

Welcome back gabriel!

© Our Site - This is the Footer

This is, I think, one of the better options you can use when creating a Handlebars site; although if you had a lot of helpers your `require` statement could get a little crazy, not to mention the browser would still be loading a large amount of files, which is not ideal.

Unfortunately there is no way to compile down helpers natively, but that begs the question whether there is a way we can implement this ourselves.

This next part is stretching the scope of the book, and will rely on some JavaScript knowledge, but it's OK if you don't understand every line, the general ideas are what's important.

Before we begin we will need to install the RequireJS package for node.js. This can be done through `npm` by running the following command from within the `js` folder:

`npm install requirejs`

When that installs, create a file named `compilehelpers.js` and enter the following:

```
var fs = require("fs");
var requirejs = require("requirejs");

fs.readdir("helpers/", function (err, files){
  if (err) {
    console.log(err);
  } else {
    var out = "define(['handlebars'], function(Handlebars) {\n";
    for (var i = 0; i < files.length; i ++) {
      var filename = files[i];
      if (filename.substr(-3) == ".js") {
        var func = requirejs("helpers/" + filename);
        var name = filename.substr(0, filename.length - 3);
```

```
        out += "\tHandlebars.helpers['" + name + "']";
        out += " = " + func.toString() + ";\n";
      }
    }

    out += "\treturn Handlebars.helpers\n";
    out += "});"

    fs.writeFileSync("precomp/helpers.js", out);
  }

});
```

Let's walk through this slowly. The first two lines include modules, this is similar to what `require.js` does except node uses a different format and the `require` command. The `fs` package is for doing things with the file system, and the RequireJS module that we just installed will be used to pull in the helpers.

In node.js, a lot of the commands are asynchronous, and as such they don't really return things. Instead you pass it a callback function, which will get called when the operation is complete. In the next line we call `readdir`, which will read all the files inside a directory and in the callback, it will pass an error variable should something go wrong, and an array of all the files in the given folder.

Next we create a variable named `out` to store the output, and we initialize it with the beginning of a module declaration that depends on Handlebars. We then cycle through the list of files making sure they are JavaScript files. This allows you to store other kinds of files like readmes or text files and not have them interfere with the command.

Inside the `if` statement, we pull in the function using RequireJS, and then write strings that will add it to the `Handlebars.helpers` object. The last line outputs the contents to the `precomp` folder into a file named `helpers.js`.

To run these files enter the following command in your terminal:

node compilehelpers.js

If all went well this will create a file named `helpers.js` inside the `precomp` folder, which contains the following code:

```
define(['handlebars'], function(Handlebars) {
  Handlebars.helpers['userfy'] = function (name) {
    var username = name.toLowerCase().replace(/ /g, "_");
    return username;
  };
  return Handlebars.helpers
});
```

You can now replace everything inside `production.js` to the following code:

```
require.config({
  paths: {
    "p": "precomp"
  },
  shim: {
    "handlebars": {
      "exports": "Handlebars"
    }
  }
});

require(['p/home', 'p/helpers', 'p/partials'], function (home,
helpers, partials) {
  var html = home({name: "Gabriel"});
  document.body.innerHTML += html;
});
```

We no longer need anything from the `helpers` folder, nor do we need to register any of the helpers once we load them. But above all that, the browser only needs to ever pull in three files at a time, minimizing a lot of the overhead that may be included.

Moving forward, you can play with editing the `compilehelper.js` to only compile the helpers needed for a certain helper. This can reduce the overall size of this file if you are working on a lot of different helpers and templates; and the same thing can be done for the partials as well, either manually with the Handlebars command or via a node app.

Logging and comments

I would like to end on a lighter note. We have covered building templates, helpers, and partials; and we have even covered how to structure larger apps. The one thing I have left to talk about is keeping your code easy to read and debug by using comments and logging.

Comment tags are a type of tag that, when the templates are compiled, the comments get removed from the output. This means they are great for storing information and messages to yourself that you don't want showing up on the final page.

To add comments you open the tag with `{{!--`, insert whatever text you want, and finally close the comment by using the `--}}` tag. These can be placed in both regular templates as well as partials; here is an example of adding comments to our `home.template` file:

```
{{> header}}
  {{!-- Convert the user's name into a username styled format --}}
  Welcome back {{userfy name}}!
{{> footer}}
```

Now logging works a bit differently. Handlebars has four different logging levels, which are as follows:

- debug
- info
- warn
- error

Each level is supposed to be more urgent than the one before it. When logging messages you get to choose the kind of message, such as whether it is just an informative message or whether it's an actual error. Then you can set a global variable defining the minimum log level to show. So, during development you can set it to 0 for debug and view all messages, but for production you can set it to 3 for error only.

The default level is error, so by default none of the other types will show up, but you can change this by altering the variable `Handlebars.logger.level` and setting it to a number between 0 and 3.

Now to do the actual logging, you have two options. The first is from anywhere you are using JavaScript, such as in a helper or in your regular code, by using the `Handlebars.logger.log` function. Here is an example of that in action:

```
define([], function(){
    return function(name) {
        var username = name.toLowerCase().replace(/ /g, "_");
        Handlebars.logger.log(1, username);
        return username;
    }
});
```

So the added line logs the username as `info`, which won't show up in production because it's log level is too low.

The other way to log things is inside a template itself, using the log helper:

```
{{log "Some Text or Object"}}
```

This is great for debugging templates, as well as just finding out what the current context is in certain locations.

By default, using this function will log with a level of 1 for info, but you can change this by editing the level property on the data object (this is the second parameter on a template). For example:

```
var html = home({name: "Gabriel"}, { data: { level: 2 }});
```

The preceding code will cause the log tag to know to log output level 2 for warn. By playing around with both this property, as well as viewing the log level, you can create templates and helpers that are very easy to debug in a pinch.

People and places you should get to know

Congratulations for making it this far. You are now an expert on both using and implementing Handlebars in your own apps. But having a set of skills or preferred libraries always requires you to subscribe to them: keeping up with changes they make, and even contributing ideas and code, advancing your environment even further. In this section we will be taking a look at both some of the people and also some of the places you should follow, so as to stay up to date and dive deeper into the Handlebars community.

The first place I would like to single out is the official Handlebars site at `http://handlebarsjs.com/`. If you have any questions or are just looking to see whether there have been any changes, this is a good place to look first (not to mention you can support the project and buy some Handlebars gear).

Official sites

Handlebars is not a large library; it's made to solve one specific issue and it does it well. With that said, I think it is the kind of library where you can take some time and learn the source. You may need to whip out a pad of paper and some markers to draw out the event flows, and maybe even debug it in JavaScript, but it's more than worth it. The compiled final source can be found at `https://raw.github.com/wycats/handlebars.js/1.0.0/dist/handlebars.js,` and while it does sometimes get a bit technical, there are some good coding concepts you can pick up, as well as learn some of Handlebars inner workings, which you can take advantage of at will.

To view the rest of the source, you can just view the entire repo here at `https://github.com/wycats/handlebars.js`. This is also where you will want to post issues, as well as make pull-requests to add new features.

Also, if you would like to learn more about `require.js` and what it can do, be sure to take a look at its official homepage `http://requirejs.org/`: it contains a lot of good information.

Community

Another resource that has become almost essential to any library is Stack Overflow. For pretty much any library around, you can ask both questions as well as contribute answers, or view solved problems. Just search for questions tagged Handlebars or even add your own at `http://stackoverflow.com/questions/tagged/handlebars`.

Another great site where I personally published two articles is NetTuts+. You can find the articles here:

- `http://bit.ly/intro_to_handlebars`
- `http://bit.ly/handlebars_behind_the_scenes`

Instant Handlebars.js

There is also a great series on Treehouse at the following links:

- `http://bit.ly/handlebars_treehouse_part_1`
- `http://bit.ly/handlebars_treehouse_part_2`
- `http://bit.ly/handlebars_treehouse_part_3`

Frameworks

A templating engine is really only one piece of a web app, and while you can really implement Handlebars into any framework, there are some that use Handlebars by default and come preconfigured with it.

Ember.js is an amazing web framework built by the creator of Handlebars, *Yehuda Katz*, and as such it embeds Handlebars deep within its core, so there is no need to pre-compile templates or load different scripts, as a lot of it is taken care of for you. It implements smart code generation, so you really only code the minimum, and I highly recommend you visit `http://emberjs.com/`, if you are serious about learning Ember.js.

Another framework, which comes pre-installed with Handlebars, is Meteor.js. Meteor is both a client and a frontend and backend framework that abstracts this connection to try and make your app update in real time, by persisting all changes to the backend and syncing any new updates to your browser at `http://www.meteor.com/`.

Twitter

Last, but not least, here are some twitter accounts you should follow to keep up with development news, including updates with Handlebars:

- `@handlebarsjs`: The official Handlebars account
- `@wycats`: Yehuda Katz's twitter account
- `@GabrielManricks`: My own personal account

[PACKT] Thank you for buying
PUBLISHING Instant Handlebars.js

About Packt Publishing

Packt, pronounced 'packed', published its first book "*Mastering phpMyAdmin for Effective MySQL Management*" in April 2004 and subsequently continued to specialize in publishing highly focused books on specific technologies and solutions.

Our books and publications share the experiences of your fellow IT professionals in adapting and customizing today's systems, applications, and frameworks. Our solution based books give you the knowledge and power to customize the software and technologies you're using to get the job done. Packt books are more specific and less general than the IT books you have seen in the past. Our unique business model allows us to bring you more focused information, giving you more of what you need to know, and less of what you don't.

Packt is a modern, yet unique publishing company, which focuses on producing quality, cutting-edge books for communities of developers, administrators, and newbies alike. For more information, please visit our website: www.packtpub.com.

Writing for Packt

We welcome all inquiries from people who are interested in authoring. Book proposals should be sent to author@packtpub.com. If your book idea is still at an early stage and you would like to discuss it first before writing a formal book proposal, contact us; one of our commissioning editors will get in touch with you.

We're not just looking for published authors; if you have strong technical skills but no writing experience, our experienced editors can help you develop a writing career, or simply get some additional reward for your expertise.

[PACKT] PUBLISHING

Instant AngularJS Starter

ISBN: 978-1-78216-676-4　　Paperback: 308 pages

A concise guide to start building dynamic web applications with AngularJS, one of the Web's most innovative JavaScript framework

1. Learn something new in an Instant! A short, fast, focused guide delivering immediate results.
2. Take a broad look at the capabilities of AngularJS, with in-depth analysis of its key features
3. See how to build a structured MVC-style application that will scale gracefully in real-world applications

Building Impressive Presentations with impress.js

ISBN: 978-1-84969-648-7　　Paperback: 124 pages

Design stunning presentations with dynamic visuals and 3D transitions that will captivate your colleagues

1. Create presentations inside the infinite canvas of modern web browsers
2. Build presentations that work anywhere, any time, and on any device
3. Build dynamic presentations with rotation, scaling, transforms, and 3D effects

Please check www.PacktPub.com for information on our titles

[PACKT] PUBLISHING

Backbone.js Cookbook

ISBN: 978-1-78216-272-8   Paperback: 282 pages

Over 80 recipes for creating outstanding web applications with Backbone.js leveraging MVC, and REST architecture principles

1. Easy-to-follow recipes to build dynamic web applications
2. Learn how to integrate with various frontend and mobile frameworks
3. Synchronize data with a RESTful backend and HTML5 local storage
4. Learn how to optimize and test Backbone applications

Learning Ext JS 4

ISBN: 978-1-84951-684-6   Paperback: 434 pages

SEncha Ext JS for a beginner

1. Learn the basics and create your first classes
2. Handle data and understand the way it works, create powerful widgets and new components
3. Dig into the new architecture defined by Sencha and work on real world projects

Please check **www.PacktPub.com** for information on our titles

Printed in Germany
by Amazon Distribution
GmbH, Leipzig